I0815494

★★★★★
MLB TEAMS

New York YANKEES

KENNY ABDO

Fly!
An Imprint of Abdo Zoom
abdobooks.com

abdobooks.com

Published by Abdo Zoom, a division of ABDO, P.O. Box 398166, Minneapolis, Minnesota 55439. Fly!™ is a trademark and logo of Abdo Zoom.

Printed in the United States of America, North Mankato, Minnesota.
102025
012026

Photo Credits: Alamy, AP Images, Bridgeman Images, Getty Images, Shutterstock
Production Contributors: Kenny Abdo, Jennie Forsberg, Grace Hansen
Design Contributors: Candice Keimig, Neil Klinepier

Library of Congress Control Number: 2025936771

Publisher's Cataloging-in-Publication Data

Names: Abdo, Kenny, author.
Title: New York Yankees / by Kenny Abdo
Description: Minneapolis, Minnesota : Abdo Zoom, 2026 | Series: MLB teams | Includes online resources and index.
Identifiers: ISBN 9798384940272 (lib. bdg.) | ISBN 9798384941033 (ebook) | ISBN 9798384941415 (read-to-me ebook)
Subjects: LCSH: New York Yankees (Baseball team)--Juvenile literature. | Baseball teams--Juvenile literature. | Professional sports--Juvenile literature. | Sports franchises--Juvenile literature. | Major League Baseball (Organization)--Juvenile literature.
Classification: DDC 796.357--dc23

Table of CONTENTS

YANKEES

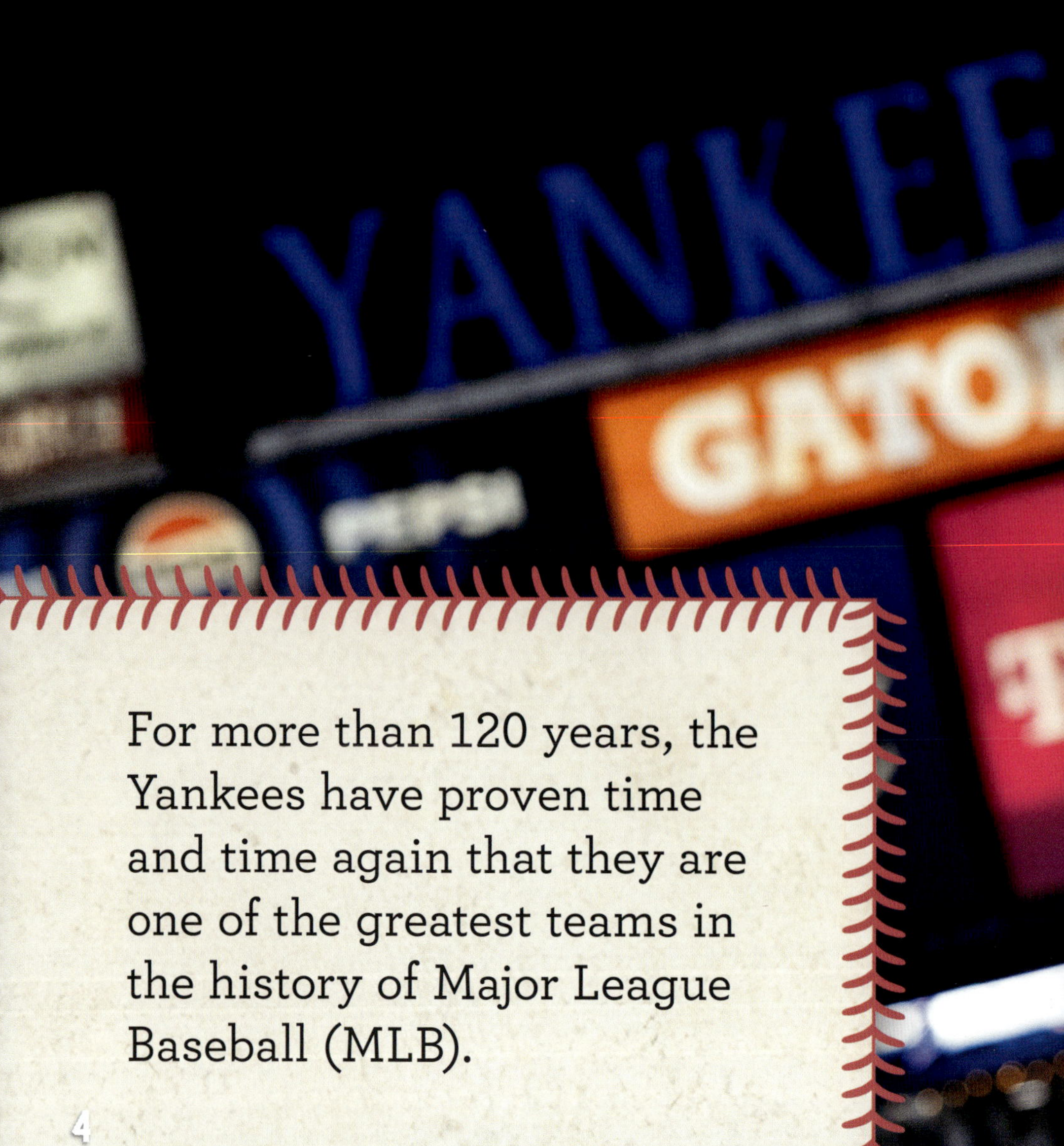

For more than 120 years, the Yankees have proven time and time again that they are one of the greatest teams in the history of Major League Baseball (MLB).

Rawlings
Est. 1887
99

With 27 World Series titles, the Yankees have earned their pinstripes and shine brighter than Times Square!

STARR
INSURANCE
YORK

BATTER UP!

The team began play as the New York Highlanders in 1903. They found success right away, winning 92 games in their second season. By 1913, the team moved from high up in Hilltop Park down to the Polo Grounds. They also got a new name: the Yankees.

NY

In the 1920s, stars such as Babe Ruth and Lou Gehrig helped the Yankees rise to greatness. The year 1923 was an especially great one for the team. The Yankees moved into their brand new stadium in the Bronx, Ruth hit 41 home runs for the season, and the team got its first of many World Series wins.

PHILA
CHIGO
WASH
DETRT 0
BOST 0
CLEVE 0 0 0 0
YANKS 0 0 0
AT BAT
5
STRIKES
UMPIRES • PLATE
BASES

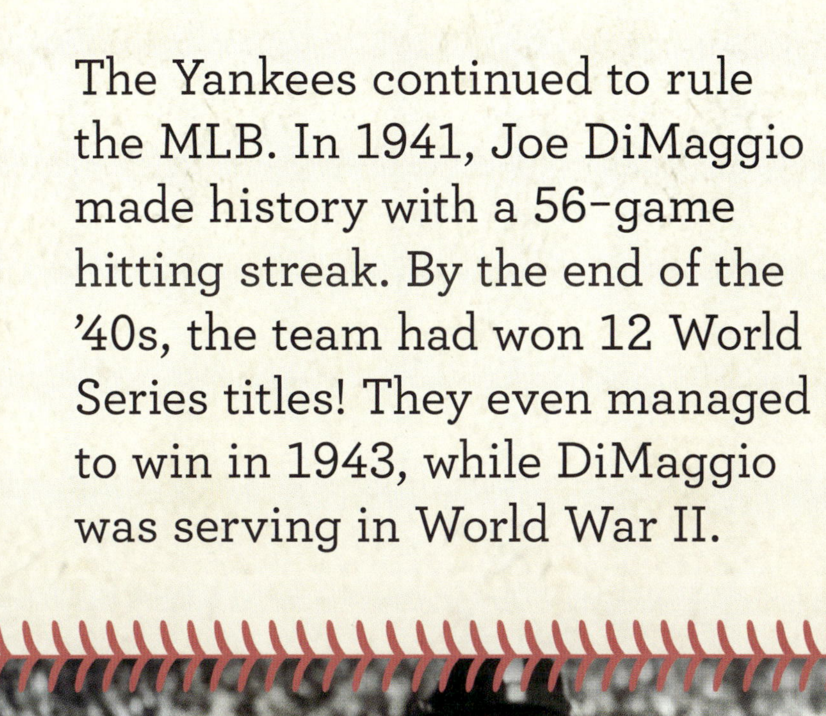

The Yankees continued to rule the MLB. In 1941, Joe DiMaggio made history with a 56-game hitting streak. By the end of the '40s, the team had won 12 World Series titles! They even managed to win in 1943, while DiMaggio was serving in World War II.

GRAND SLAMS

The year 1953 marked the Yankees fifth consecutive World Series win, the longest streak in MLB history. In 1956, Mickey Mantle hit 52 home runs and won the **Triple Crown**! Yogi Berra stood out in the 1950s as an exceptional hitter and catcher and won multiple MVP awards.

The 1970s brought the Yankees more wins. In 1977, the team defeated the Dodgers in six games to win the World Series. Reggie Jackson hit three home runs in Game 6 to help clinch the title!

In the 1990s, the Yankees became a powerhouse again. From 1996 to 2000, Derek Jeter helped lead the team to four World Series wins. The Yankees won their 27th championship in 2009, the most in MLB history!

CASIO
HESS
metli
NewYork-Pres
Official Hospital

Aaron Judge made history in 2022 by hitting 62 home runs, the most in **American League** (**AL**) history!

The Yankees won the **AL pennant** in 2024. It was the team's first since 2009. However, they moved on to lose the World Series to the Dodgers.

99

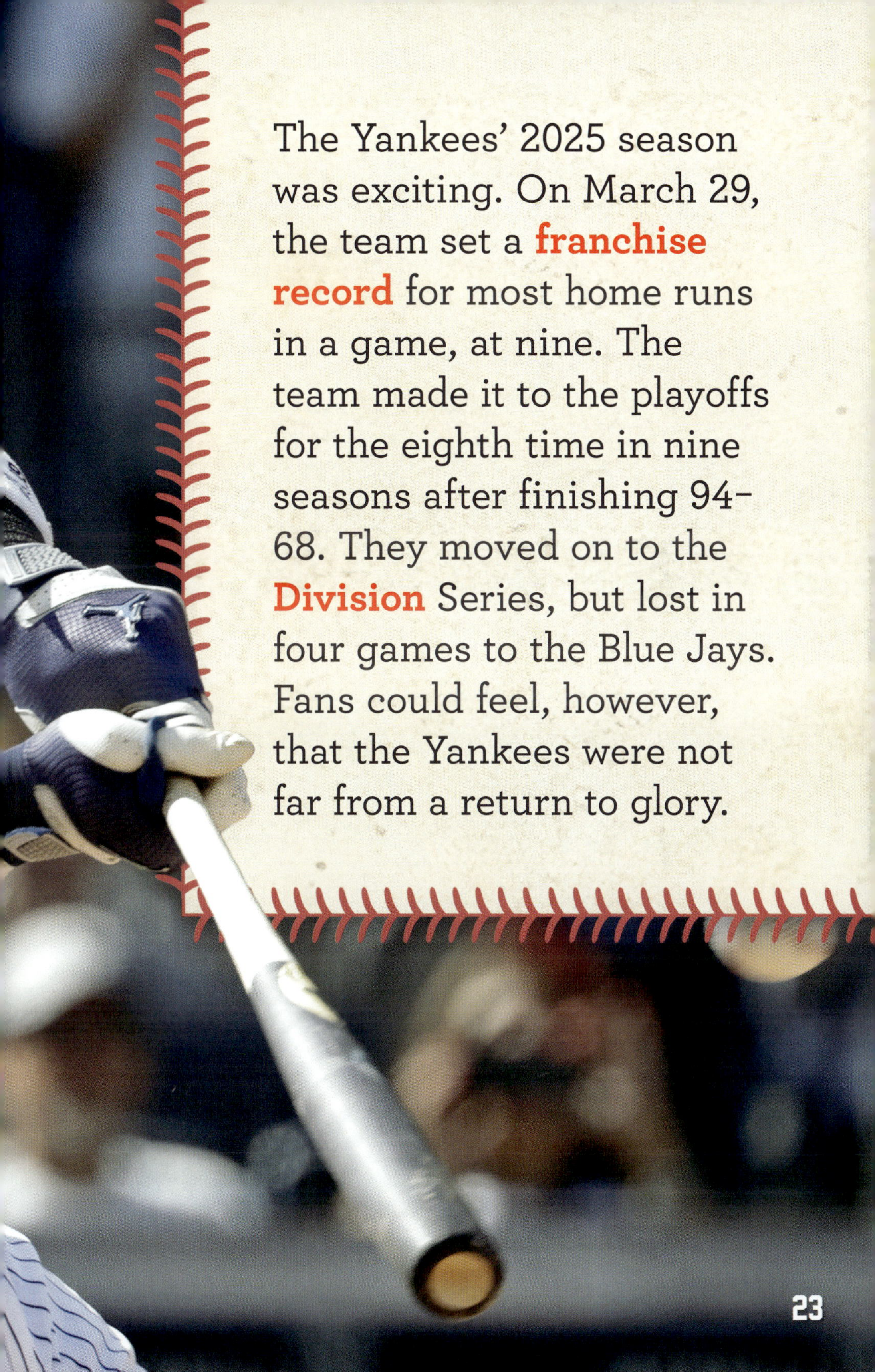

The Yankees' 2025 season was exciting. On March 29, the team set a **franchise record** for most home runs in a game, at nine. The team made it to the playoffs for the eighth time in nine seasons after finishing 94–68. They moved on to the **Division** Series, but lost in four games to the Blue Jays. Fans could feel, however, that the Yankees were not far from a return to glory.

HALL OF FAME

Babe Ruth's strong bat earned him many nicknames. The Sultan of Swat hit 714 home runs in his career and once blasted a ball a **record** 575 feet (175 m)! Ruth helped the Yankees win four World Series. He is one of the most famous players in baseball history. Ruth was **inducted** into the Baseball Hall of Fame in 1936.

NY
NY

Joe DiMaggio is known for his 56-game hitting streak in 1941, a **record** that still stands today. Many consider the feat to be unbreakable.

During his famous streak, DiMaggio struck out just 5 times, showing his amazing bat control. He helped the Yankees win nine World Series titles and was named to the Baseball Hall of Fame in 1955.

Derek Jeter connected more than 3,400 hits and led the Yankees to five World Series wins. The famous shortstop was known for his leadership and clutch plays, including his legendary "The Flip" play in the 2001 playoffs. Jeter was **inducted** into the Baseball Hall of Fame in 2020.

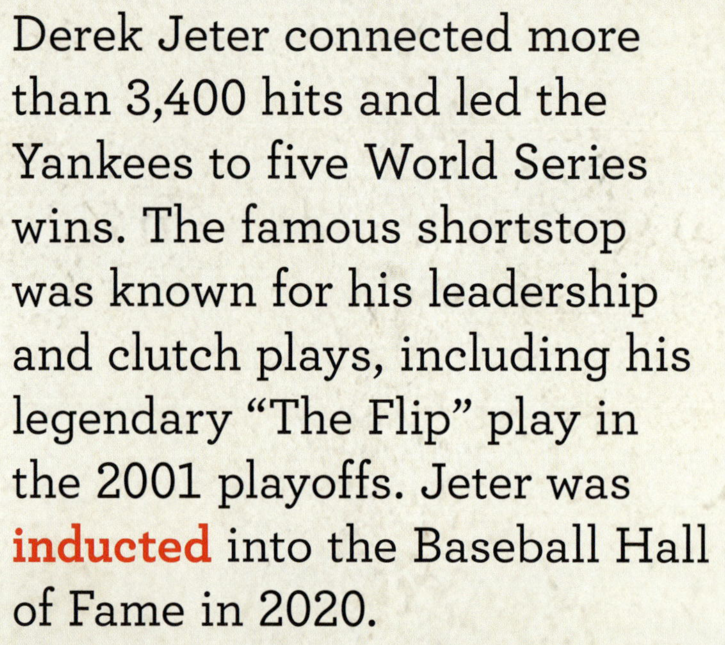

GLOSSARY

American League (AL) – one of two 15-team leagues that make up MLB.

division – a number of teams grouped together in a sport for competitive purposes.

franchise – a sports organization, including the top-level team and all minor league affiliates.

inducted – brought in as a member.

pennant – a title given to the team that wins the AL or National League (NL) championship in baseball.

record – the top achievement by a team or player that no one has done before; the total number of wins and losses a team has in a season.

Triple Crown – an achievement earned when leading the league in batting average, home runs, and RBIs in the same season.

ONLINE RESOURCES

To learn more about the New York Yankees, please visit **abdobooklinks.com** or scan this QR code. These links are routinely monitored and updated to provide the most current information available.

INDEX